My First **Action Words** Picture Dictionary

ENGLISH - RUSSIAN

Designed and edited by : Anna Stoker

Translated by : Yernar Tursynbay

ENGLISH - RUSSIAN

My First
Action Words
Picture Dictionary

© Publishers

ISBN : 978 93 83526 85 7

Published by
WigWam
An imprint of **Star Publishers Distributors**
F-31, Okhla Industrial Area Phase I
New Delhi - 110 020
email : starprint@starpublic.com

First Edition : 2022

Printed at : Star Print-O-Bind, New Delhi-110 020 (India)

This dictionary has been published in the following languages:
Arabic, Bengali, Bulgarian, Cantonese, Croatian, Czech, Farsi, French, Gujarati, Hindi
Hungarian, Italian, Korean, Latvian, Levantine, Lithuanian, Mandarin, Pashto, Polish, Portuguese
Punjabi, Romanian, Russian, Slovak, Spanish, Tamil, Urdu and Vietnamese.

abandon

Покидать
pokidat'

absent

Отсутствовать
otsutstvovat'

absorb

Поглощать
pogloshchat'

accelerate

Ускоряться
uskorjat'sya

accept

Принимать
prinimat'

access

Получать доступ
poluchat' dostup

accompany

Сопровождать
soprovozhdat'

accuse

Обвинять
obvinyat'

ache

Болеть
bolet'

achieve

Достигать
dostigat'

acquire

Приобретать
priobretat'

act

Действовать
deystvovat'

add

Добавлять
dobavlyat'

adjust

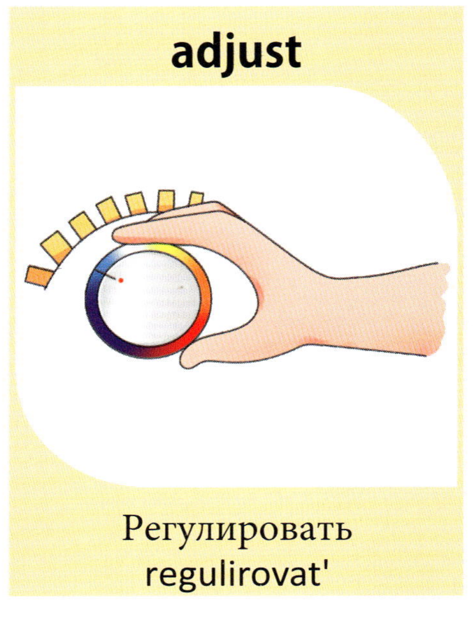

Регулировать
regulirovat'

admire

Восхищаться
voshishchat'sya

admit

Признавать
priznavat'

adopt

Усыновлять
usynovlyat'

adore

Обожать
obozhat'

advance

Продвигать
prodvigat'

advise

Советовать
sovetovat'

affix

Прикреплять
prikreplyat'

afford

Иметь возможность
imet' vozmozhnost'

agree

Соглашаться
soglashat'sya

aid

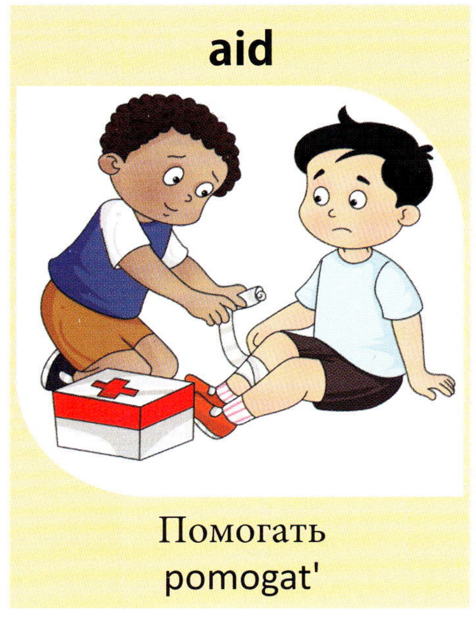

Помогать
pomogat'

aim

Целиться
tsel'sya

align

Выравнивать
vyravnnivat'

allow

Разрешать
razreshat'

alter

Изменять
izmenyzt'

amaze

Удивлять
udivlyat'

amuse

Развлекать
razvlekat'

analyse

US English **analyze**

Анализировать
analizirovat'

anger

Злиться
zlit'sya

announce

Объявлять
ob"yavlyat'

annoy

Раздражать
razdrazhat'

answer

Отвечать
otvechat'

apologise

US English **apologize**

Извиняться
izvinyat'sya

appear

Появляться
poyavlyat'sya

applaud

Аплодировать
aplodirovat'

apply

Применять
primenyat'

appoint

Назначать
naznachat'

approach

Подходить
podkhodit'

approve

Утверждать
utverzhdat'

argue

Спорить
sporit'

arise

Вставать
vstavat'

arrange

Выстраивать
vystraivat'

arrest

Арестовывать
arestovyvat'

arrive

Прибывать
pribyvat'

ask

Спрашивать
sprashivat'

assemble

Собирать
sobirat'

assist

Помогать
pomogat'

attach

Прикреплять
prikreplyat'

attack

Атаковать
atakovat'

attain

Достигать
dostigat'

attempt

Пытаться
pytat'sya

attend

Присутствовать
prisutstvovat'

attract

Привлекать
privlekat'

avoid

Избегать
izbegat'

await

Ждать
zhdat'

awake

Просыпаться
prosypat'sya

Bb

bake

Печь
pech'

balance

Балансировать
balansirovat'

ban

Запрещать
zapreshchat'

bandage

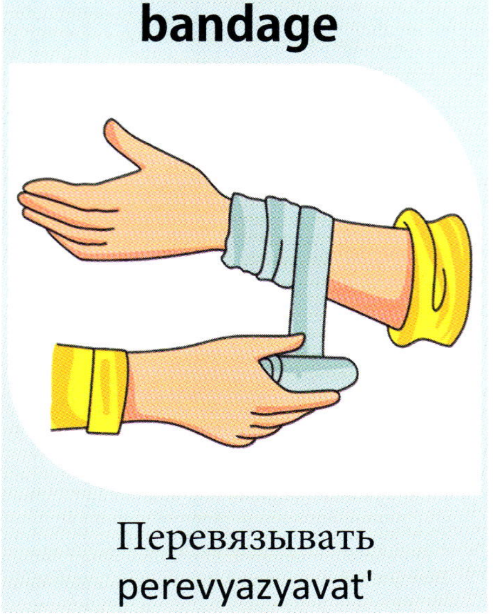

Перевязывать
perevyazyavat'

barbecue

Жарить на углях
zharit' na uglyah

bargain

Торговаться
torgovat'sya

bark

Лаять
layat'

bathe

Купаться
kupat'sya

battle

Сражаться
srazhat'sya

bear

Носить
nosit'

beat

Ударять
udaryat'

become

Становиться
stanovi'tsya

beg

Умолять
umolyat'

begin

Начинать
nachinat'

behave

Вести себя
vesti sebya

believe

Верить
verit'

belong

Принадлежать
prinadlezhat'

bend

Сгибаться
sgibat'sya

bet

Делать ставку
delat' stavku

beware

Остерегаться
osteregat'sya

bicycle

Ездить на велосипеде
ezdit' na velosipede

bite

Кусать
kusat'

blame

Обвинять
obvinyat'

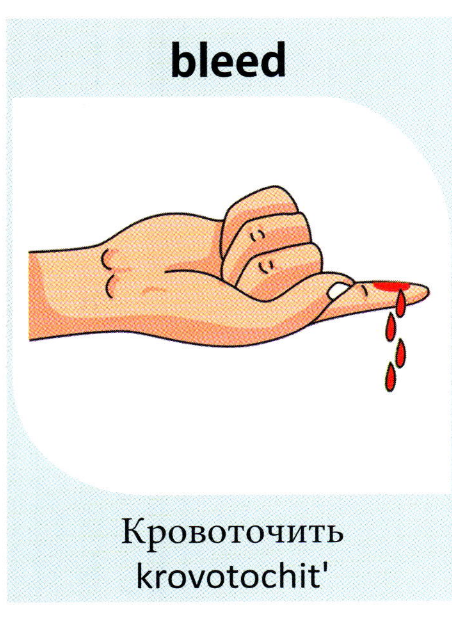

bleed

Кровоточить
krovotochit'

blend

Смешивать
smeshivat'

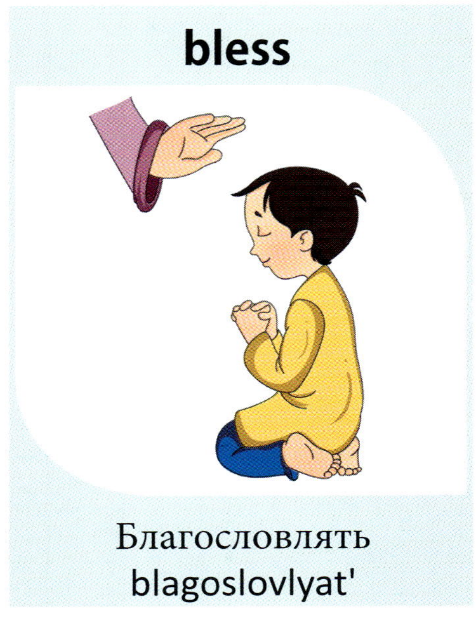

bless

Благословлять
blagoslovlyat'

blink

Моргать
morgat'

block

Блокировать
blokirovat'

bloom

Цвести
tsvesti

blow

Дуть
dut'

blow up

Надувать
naduvat''

blush

Краснеть
krasnet'

board

Садиться
sadit'dya

boast

Хвастаться
khvastat'sya

boil

Кипятить
kipyatit'

book

Брать билет
brat' bilet

borrow

Занимать
zanimat'

bother

Беспокоить
bespokoit'

bounce

Подпрыгивать
podprygivat'

bow

Кланяться
klanyat'sya

bowl

US English **pitch**

Подавать мяч
podavat' myach

box

Боксировать
boksirovat'

break

Ломать
lomati

break down

Ломаться
lomat'sya

break in

Вламываться
vlamyvat'sya

break out

Сбегать
sbegat'

breathe

Дышать
dyshat'

bring

Приносить
prinosit'

bring back

Возвращать
vozvrashchat'

bring up

Воспитывать
vospityvat'

browse

Просматривать
prosmatrivat'

brush

Чистить щеткой
chistit' shchetka

buckle

Застегивать пряжку
zastegivat' pryazhka

budge

Сдвинуть с места
sdvinut' s mesta

build

Строить
stroit'

bully

Задирать
zadirat'

bump

Ударяться
udaryat'sya

burn

Гореть
goret'

burst

Лопаться
lopat'sya

bury

Закапывать
zakapyvat'

button

Застегивать
zastegivat'

buy

Покупать
pokupat'

cage

Сажать в клетку
sazhat' v kletku

calculate

Рассчитать
rasschitat'

call

Звонить
zvonit'

camp

Устраивать лагерь
ustraivat' lager'

can

Консервировать
konservirovat'

care

Заботиться
zabotit'sya

carry

Нести
nesti

carve

Вырезать
vyrezat'

catch

Ловить
lovit'

catch up

Настигать
nastigat'

celebrate

Праздновать
prazdnovat'

change

Менять
menyat'

charge

Заряжать
zaryazhat'

chase

Гнаться
gnat'sya

chat

Беседовать
besedovat'

cheat

Жульничать
zhul'nichat'

check

Проверять
proveryat'

check in

Регистрироваться
registrirovat'sya

check up

Проверять
proveryat'

cheer

Радоваться
radovat'sya

chew

Жевать
zhevat'

chip

Обтесывать
obtesyvat'

chirp

Щебетать
shchebetat'

choose

Выбирать
vybirat'

chop

Нарезать
narezat'

chuckle

Хихикать
khikhikat'

circle

Обводить кружком
obvodit' kruzhkom

claim

Требовать
trebovat'

clap

Хлопать
khlopat'

clean

Чистить
chistit'

clear

Очищать
ochishchat'

click

US English **snap**

Нажимать
nazhimat'

climb

Взбираться
vzbirat'sya

cling

Цепляться
tseplyat'sya

clip

Зажимать
zazhimat'

close

Закрывать
zakryvat'

cluck

Кудахтать
kudakhtat'

coach

Тренировать
trenirovat'

coil

Извиваться
izvivat'sya

collapse

Рухнуть
ruhnut'

collect

Собирать
sobirat'

collide

Сталкиваться
stalkivat'sya

colour

US English **color**

Раскрашивать
raskrashivat'

comb

Расчесывать
raschesyvat'

come

Приходить
prikhodit'

come in

Входить
vhodit'

come out

Выходить
vyhodit'

commence

Начинать
nachinat'

commute

Ездить на работу
ezdit' na rabotu

compete

Соревноваться
sorevnovat'sya

complain

Жаловаться
zhalovat'sya

conduct

Проводить
provodit'

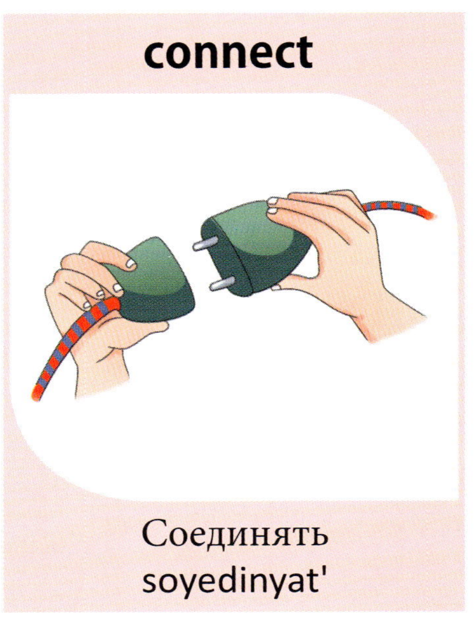

connect

Соединять
soyedinyat'

consult

Консультировать
konsul'tirovat'

cook

Готовить
gotovit'

cool

Охлаждать
ohlazhdat'

copy

Копировать
kopirovat'

cough

Кашлять
kashelyat'

count

Считать
schitat'

cover

Прикрывать
prikryvat'

crack

Трескаться
treskat'sya

crash

Разбиться
razbirat'sya

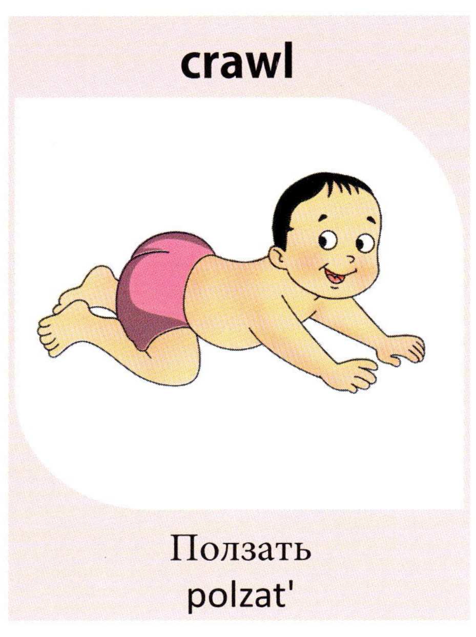

crawl

Ползать
polzat'

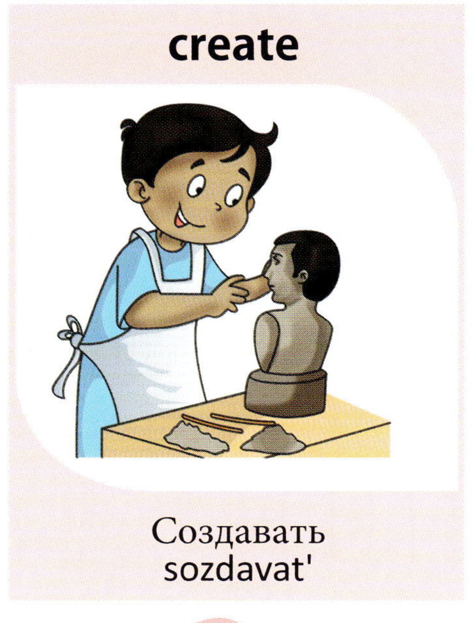

create

Создавать
sozdavat'

creep

Красться
krast'sya

croak

Квакать
kvakat'

cross

Переходить
perehodit'

cross out

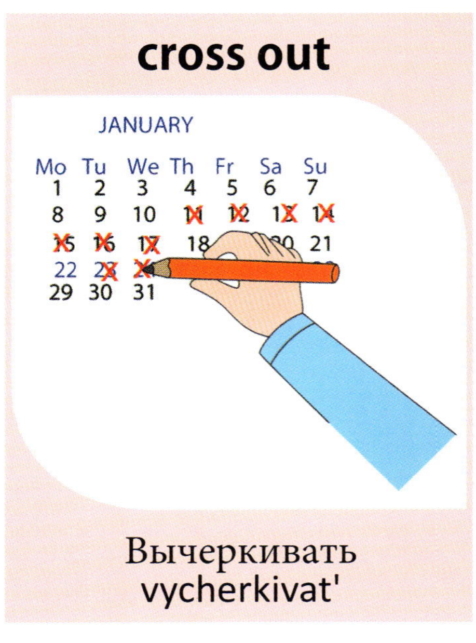

Вычеркивать
vycherkivat'

crouch

Припасть к земле
pripast' k zemle

crow

Кукарекать
kukarekat'

crowd

Толпиться
tolpit'sya

crumble

Крошить
kroshit'

cry

Плакать
plakat'

cuddle

Обнимать
obnimat'

curl

Завивать
zavivat'

cut

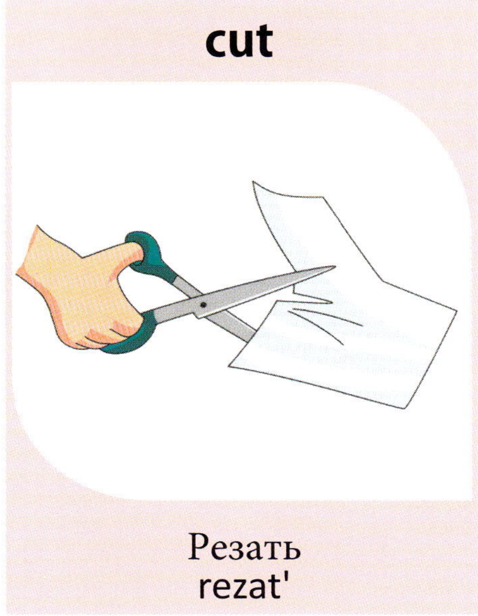

Резать
rezat'

cut down

Вырубать
vyrubat'

Dd

damage

Повреждать
povrezhdat'

dance

Танцевать
tantstvat'

dangle

Свисать
svisat'

darn

Штопать
shtopat'

dash

Мчаться
mchat'sya

decide

Решать
reshat'

decorate

Украшать
ukrashat'

defend

Защищать
zashchishchat'

deliver

Доставлять
dostavlyat'

design

Проектировать
proektirovat'

destroy

Разрушать
razrushat'

dial

Набирать номер
nabirat' nomer

dice

Нарезать
narezat'

dig

Копать
kopat'

dip

Окунать
okunat'

disappear

Пропадать
propadat'

disappoint

Разочаровать
razocharovat'

discard

Выбрасывать
vybrasyvat'

discover

Обнаруживать
obnaruzhivat'

dive

Нырять
nutyat'

divide

Разделять
razdelyat'

do

Делать
delat'

drag

Тащить
tashchit'

draw

Рисовать
risovat'

dream

Мечтать
mechtat'

dress

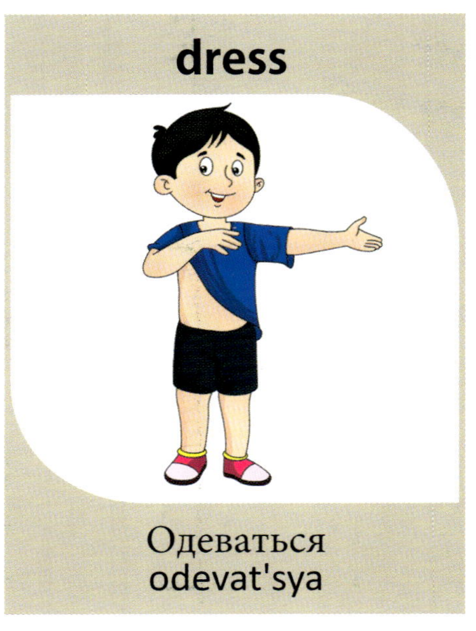

Одеваться
odevat'sya

drift

Дрейфовать
dreyfovat'

drill

Сверлить
sverlit'

drink

Пить
pit'

drive

Водить
vodit'

drop

Ронять
ronyat'

dry

Сушить
sushit'

Ee

earn

Зарабатывать
zarabatyvat'

eat

Есть
yest'

elect

Избирать
izbirat'

embrace

Обнимать
obnimat'

empty

Опустошить
opustoshit'

enclose

Огораживать
ogorazhivat'

encourage

Поощрять
pooshchryat'

enjoy

Наслаждаться
naslazhdat'sya

enter

Входить
vhodit'

entertain

Развлекать
razvlekat'

erase

Стирать
stirat'

escape

Бежать
bezhat'

examine

Осматривать
osmatrivat'

excite

Возбуждать
vozbuzhdat'

exercise

Упражняться
uprazhnyat'sya

explain

Объяснять
ob"yasnyat'

explore

Исследовать
issledovat'

Ff

fail

Проваливать
provalivat'

faint

Падать в обморок
padat' v obmorok

fall

Падать
padat'

fall asleep

Засыпать
zasypat'

feed

Кормить
kormit'

feel

Чувствовать
chuvstvovat'

fetch

Приносить
prinosit'

fight

Драться
drat'sya

fill

Наполнять
napolnyat'

find

Находить
nakhodit'

fish

Рыбачить
rybachit'

fit

Примерять
primeryat'

fix

Исправлять
ispravlyat'

flap

Взмахивать
vzmakhivat'

flash

Сверкать
sverkat'

flee

Убегать
ubegat'

fling

Бросать
brosat'

flip

Подбрасывать
podbrasyvat'

float

Плавать
plavat'

flood

Затоплять
zatoplyat'

fly

Летать
letat'

fold

Складывать
skladyvat'

follow

Следовать
sledovat'

forbid

Запрещать
zapreshchat'

forget

Забывать
zabyvat'

freeze

Замерзать
zamerzat'

frighten

Напугать
napugat'

frown

Хмуриться
khmurit'sya

fry

Жарить
zharit'

Gg

gain

Набирать
nabirat'

gallop

Галопировать
galopirovat'

gape

Зевать
zevat'

garden

Заниматься садом
zanimat'sya sadom

gargle

Полоскать горло
poloskat' gorlo

gasp

Дышать с трудом
dyshat' s trudom

gather

Собирать
sobirat'

gaze

Наблюдать
nablyudat'

gesture

Жестикулировать
zhestikulirovat'

get

Получать
poluchat'

get across

Переходить
perekhodit'

get down

Спускаться
spuskat'sya

get dressed

Одеваться
odevat'sya

get off

Слезать
slezat'

get on

Садиться
sadit'sya

get over

Преодолевать
preodolevat'

get up

Вставать
vstavat'

giggle

Хихикать
khikhikat'

give

Давать
davat'

go

Идти
idti

gobble

Пожирать
pozhirat'

grab

Схватывать
skhvatyvat'

grate

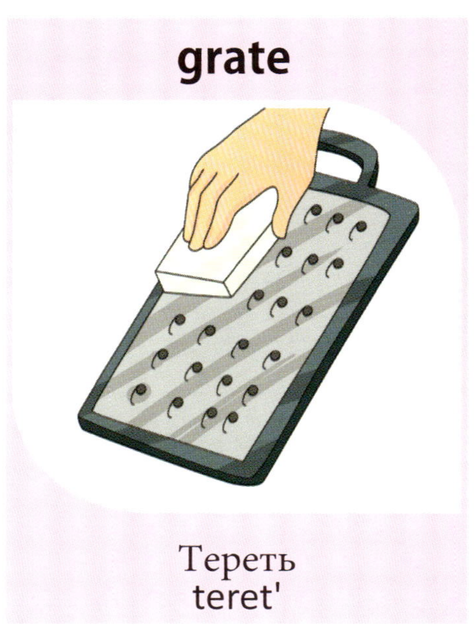

Тереть
teret'

grease

Смазывать
smazyvat'

greet

Приветствовать
privetstvovat'

grill

Жарить на гриле
zharit' na gril'

grin

Ухмыляться
ukhmylyat'sya

grind

Молоть
molot'

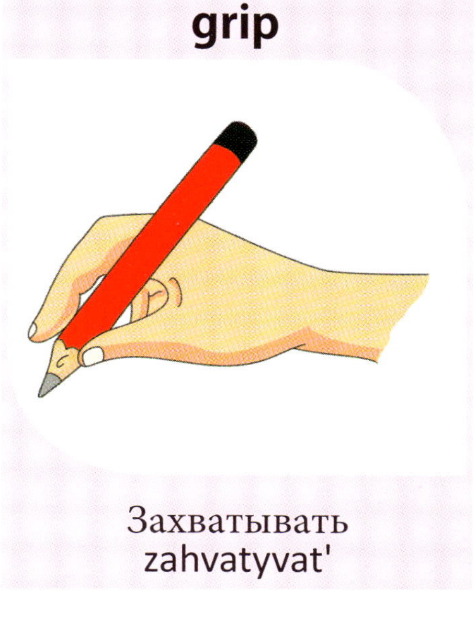

grip

Захватывать
zahvatyvat'

grow

Расти
rasti

growl

Рычать
rychat'

grunt

Хрюкать
khryukat'

guard

Сторожить
storozhit'

guess

Гадать
gadat'

guide

Направлять
napravlyat'

Hh

halt

Останавливать
ostanavlivat'

halve

Делить пополам
delit' popolam

hammer

Стучать молотком
stuchat' molotok

handcuff

Надевать наручники
nfdevat' naruchniki

hang

Висеть
viset'

harvest

Собрать урожай
sobrat' urozhay

hatch

Вылупиться
vylupit'sya

hate

Ненавидеть
nenavidet'

heap

Нагромождать
nagromozhdat'

hear

Слушать
slushat'

heat

Нагревать
nagrevat'

help

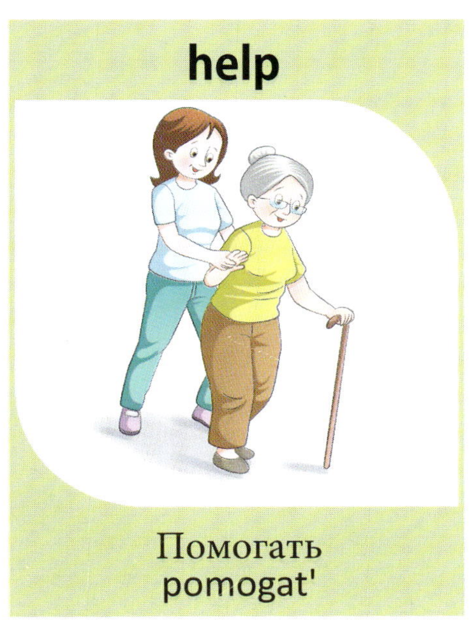

Помогать
pomogat'

hide

Прятаться
pryatat'sya

hike

Путешествовать пешком
puteshestvovat' peshkom

hiss

Шипеть
shipet'

hit

Ударять
udaryat'

hoist

Поднимать
podnimat'

hold

Держать
derzhat'

honk

Гудеть
gudet'

hop

Прыгать
prygat'

host

Принимать гостей
prinimat' gostei

hover

Зависать
zavisat'

huddle

Собираться
sobirat'sya

hug

Обнимать
obnimat'

hum

Напевать
napevat'

hurt

Повреждать
povrezhdat'

Ii

imagine

Представлять
predstavlyat'

injure

Ранить
ranit'

insert

Вкладывать
vkladyvat'

inspect

Осматривать
osmatrivat'

install

Устанавливать
ustanavlivat'

instruct

Обучать
obuchat'

interview

Брать интервью
brat' interv'yu

introduce

Представлять
predstavlyat'

invent

Изобретать
izobretat'

iron

Гладить
gladit'

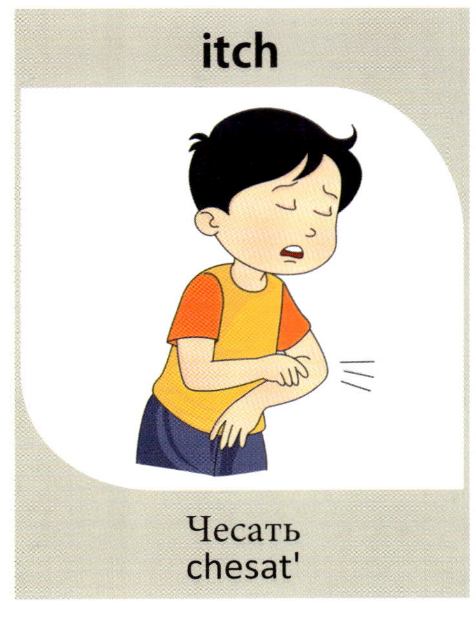

itch

Чесать
chesat'

Jj

jam

Заклинивать
zakllinivat'

jingle

Звенеть
zvenet'

jog

Бегать
begat'

join

Присоединяться
prisoyedinyat'sya

joke

Шутить
shutit'

jolt

Трястись
tryastis'

jostle

Толкаться
tolkat'sya

jot

Быстро писать
bystro ppisat'

juggle

Жонглировать
zhonglirovat'

jumble

Смешать
smeshat'

jump

Прыгать
prygat'

Kk

keep

Держать
derzhat'

keep off

Держаться подальше
derzhat'sya podal'she

kick

Пинать
pinat'

kindle

Разжечь
razzhech'

kiss

Целовать
tselovat'

knead

Месить
mesit'

kneel

Становиться на колени
stanovit'sya na koleni

knit

Вязать
vyazat'

knock

Стучать
stuchat'

knock down

Сбить
sbit'

know

Знать
znat'

L l

land

Приземляться
prizemlyat'sya

laugh

Смеяться
smeyat'sya

lay

Нести
nesti

lead

Вести
vesti

leak

Утекать
utekat'

lean

Прислоняться
prislonyat'sya

leap

Выпрыгивать
vyprygivat'

learn

Учиться
uchit'sya

leave

Покинуть
pokinut'

lend

Давать в долг
davat' v dolg

let go

Отпустить
otpustit'

let in

Впустить
vpustit'

lie

Врать
lozh'

lift

Поднимать
podnimat'

light

Зажечь
zazhech'

like

Нравиться
nravit'sya

listen

Слушать
slushat'

load

Загружать
zagruzhat'

lock

Запирать
zapirat'

look

Смотреть
smotret'

loosen

Освобождать
osvobozhdat'

lose

Терять
teryat'

love

Любить
lyubit'

Mm

mail

Отправить письмо
otpravit' pis'mo

make

Делать
delat'

manufacture

Производить
proizvodit'

march

Маршировать
marshirovat'

mark

Отмечать
otmechat'

marry

Вступать в брак
vstupat' v brak

mash

Толочь
toloch'

match

Совпадать
sovpadat'

measure

Измерять
izmeryat'

meet

Встречать
vstrechat'

melt

Таять
tayat'

mend

Исправлять
ispravlyat'

mew

Мяукать
myaukat'

milk

Доить
doit'

mime

Подрожать
podrozhat'

mince

Нарубить
nrubit'

mix

Смешивать
smeshivat'

model

Позировать
pozirovat'

mop

Мыть шваброй
myt' shvabroi

mount

Взбираться
vzbirat'sya

move

Передвигать
peredvigat'

mow

Косить
kosit'

munch

Жевать
zhevat'

Nn

nail

Прибивать
nogot'

name

Давать имя
davat' imya

nap

Дремать
dremat'

neigh

Ржать
rzhat'

net

Ловить сетью
lovit' set'yu

nibble

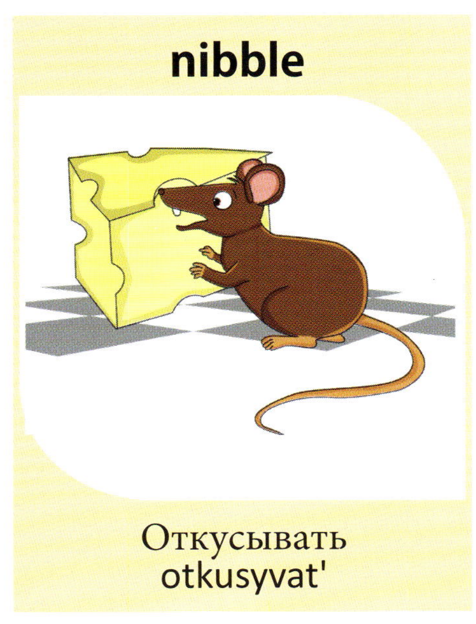

Откусывать
otkusyvat'

nip

Укусить
ukusit'

nod

Кивать
kivat'

notice

Уведомлять
uvedomlyat'

nudge

Подталкивать
podtalkivat'

nurse

Ухаживать
uhazhivat'

Oo

obey

Подчиняться
podchinyat'sya

occupy

Занимать
zanimat'

offer

Предлагать
predlagat'

oil

Залить масло
zalit' maslo

open

Открывать
otkryvat'

operate

Работать
rabotat'

order

Заказывать
zakazyvat'

overtake

Обгонять
obgonyat'

overturn

Переворачиваться
perevorachivat'sya

owe

Задолжать
zadolzhat'

own

Владеть
vladet'

Pp

pack

Упаковать
upakovat'

paddle

Грести
gresti

paint

Покрасить
pokrasit'

park

Припарковать
priparkovat'

part

Расходиться
raskhodit'sya

pass

Передать
pererdat'

paste

Вставить
vstavit'

pat

Поглаживать
poglazhivat'

patch

Латать
latat'

patrol

Патрулировать
patrulirovat'

pave

Прокладывать
prokladyvat'

paw

Хватать
khvatat'

pay

Платить
platit'

peck

Клевать
klevat'

pedal

Нажимать на педали
nazhimat' na pedali

peel

Чистить
chistit'

peep

Подглядывать
podglyadyvat'

peg

Прикреплять
prikreplyat'

perch

Усесться
usest'sya

perform

Исполнять
ispolnyat'

phone

Звонить
zvonit'

photograph

Фотографироваться
fotografirovat'sya

pick

Выбирать
vybirat'

### pick up	### picnic	### pierce
		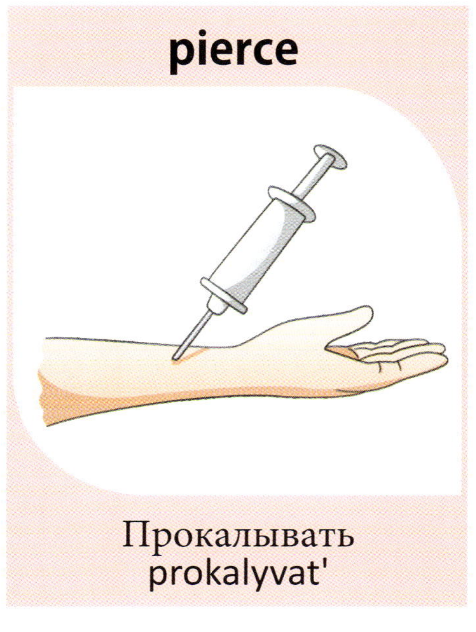
Подобрать podobrat'	Устраивать пикник ustraivat' piknik	Прокалывать prokalyvat'
### pile	### pin	### pinch

Сваливать в кучу svalivat' v kuchu	Прикалывать prokalyvat'	Ущипнуть ushchipnut'
### place	### plan	### plant

Поставить postavit'	Планировать planirovat'	Сажать растение sazhat' rasteniye

play

Играть
igrat'

plough

Пахать
pakhat'

pluck

Срывать
sryvat'

plug

Вставлять
vstavlyat'

point

Указывать
ukazyvat'

poke

Тыкать
tykat'

polish

Натирать
natirat'

pollute

Загрязнять
zagryaznyat'

pose

Позировать
pozirovat'

pour

Наливать
nalivat'

powder

Пудриться
pudrit'sya

praise

Хвалить
khvalit'

pray

Молиться
molit'sya

press

Нажимать
nazhimat'

print

Распечатать
raspechatat'

protect

Защищать
zashchishchat'

pull

Тянуть
tyanut'

pump

Качать
kachat'

punch

Ударить кулаком
udarit' kulakom

punish

Наказывать
nakazyvat'

push

Толкать
tolkat'

Qq

quack

Крякать
kryakat'

quarrel

Ссориться
ssorit'sya

quarter

Разделить на четыре
razdelit' na chetyre

quench

Утолять жажду
utolyat' zhazhdu

question

Спрашивать
sprashivat'

queue

Стоять в очереди
stoyat' v ocheredi

quit

Покидать
pokidat'

quiz

Опрашивать
oprashivat'

Rr

race

Состязаться
sosotyazat'sya

rain

Идет дождь
idet dozhd'

raise

Поднимать
podnimat'

rake

Разгребать
razgrebat'

ram

Налетать на
naletat' na

reach

Достигать
dostigat'

read

Читать
chitat'

receive

Получать
poluchat'

recline

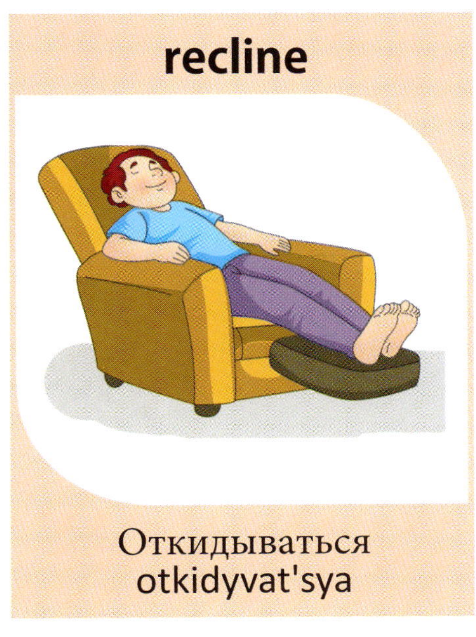

Откидываться
otkidyvat'sya

record

Записывать
zapisyvat'

recycle

Перерабатывать
pererabatyvat'

reflect

Отражать
otrazhat'

refuse

Отказывать
otkazyvat'

release

Выпускать
vypuskat'

remember

Помнить
pomnit'

repair

Ремонтировать
remontirovat'

report

Сообщать
soobshchat'

request

Запрашивать
zaprashivat'

rescue

Спасать
spasat'

respect

Уважать
uvazhat'

rest

Отдыхать
otdykhat'

return

Возвращать
vozvrashchat'

ride

Ездить
ezdit'

ring

Звенеть
zvenet'

ring up

Позвонить
pozvonit'

rinse

Промывать
promyvat'

rip

Рвать
rvat'

rise

Подниматься
pdnimat'sya

risk

Рисковать
riskovat'

roar

Рычать
rychat'

roast

Жарить
zharit'

rock

Качать
kachat'

roll

Сворачивать
svorachivat'

row

Грести
gresti

rub

Натирать
natirat'

ruffle

Рябить
ryabit'

ruin

Разрушать
razrushat'

run

Бежать
bezhat'

run after

Бежать за
bezhat' za

run into

Врезаться
vrezat'sya

rush

Торопиться
toropit'sya

Ss

sag

Провисать
provisat'

sail

Плыть
plyt'

salute

Приветствовать
privetstvovat'

save

Сохранять
sokhranyat'

scare

Напугать
napugat'

scold

Ругать
rugat'

scoop

Черпать
cherpat'

score

Набрать балов
nabrat' balov

scratch

Царапать
tsarapat'

scratch out

Вычеркивать
vycherkivat'

scream

Кричать
krichat'

screw

Завинчивать
zavinchivat'

scrub

Тереть
teret'

seal

Запечатать
zapechatat'

see

Видеть
videt'

seek

Искать
iskat'

select

Выбирать
vybirat'

Продавать
prodavat'

Отправлять
otpravlyat'

Отделять
otdelyat'

Служить
sluzhit'

Устанавливать
ustanavlivat'

Шить
shit'

Затемнять
zatemnyat'

Встряхивать
vstryakhivat'

Формировать
formirovat'

share	**sharpen**	**shave**

Делиться delit'sya	Точить tochit'	Бриться brit'sya
shear	**shell**	**shelter**

Стричь strich'	Снимать шелуху snimat' shelukhu	Укрываться ukryvat'sya
shift	**shine**	**shiver**

Сдвигать sdvigat'	Светить svetit'	Дрожать drozhat'

shoot

Стрелять
strelyat'

shop

Ходить за покупками
khodit' za pokupkami

shout

Кричать
krichat'

shovel

Копать
kopat'

show

Показывать
pokazyvat'

shower

Принимать душ
prinimat' dush

shut

Закрывать
zakryvat'

sign

Подписывать
podpisyvat'

signal

Сигналить
signalit'

sing

Петь
pet'

sink

Тонуть
tonut'

sip

Глотать
glotat'

sit

Сидеть
sidet'

skate board

Кататься на скейтборде
katat'sya na skeytborde

ski

Кататься на лыжах
katat'sya na lyzhah

skid

Заносить
zanosit'

skip

Пропускать
propuskat'

slap

Шлепать
shlepat'

slash

Косить
kosit'

sledge

Ездить на санях
ezdit' na sanyah

sleep

Спать
spat'

slice

Нарезать
narezat'

slide

Скатываться
skatyvat'sya

slip

Соскальзывать
soskal'zyvat'

slip under

Подсовывать
podsovyvat'

smash

Разгромить
razgromit'

smell

Нюхать
nyukhat'

smile

Улыбаться
ulybat'sya

snatch

Вырывать
vyryvat'

sneeze

Чихать
chikhat'

sniff

Нюхать
nyukhat'

snore

Храпеть
khrapet'

snorkel

Плавать под водой с трубкой
plavat' pod vodoi s trubkoi

snow

Идет снег
idet sneg

soak

Замачивать
zamachivat'

soar

Парить
parit'

sob

Рыдать
rydat'

sort

Сортировать
sortirovat'

sow

Сеять
seyat'

sparkle

Блестеть
blestet'

speak

Разговаривать
razgovarivat'

spill

Проливать
prolivat'

spit

Плевать
plevat'

splash

Плескаться
plekat'sya

spoil

Портить
portit'

spray

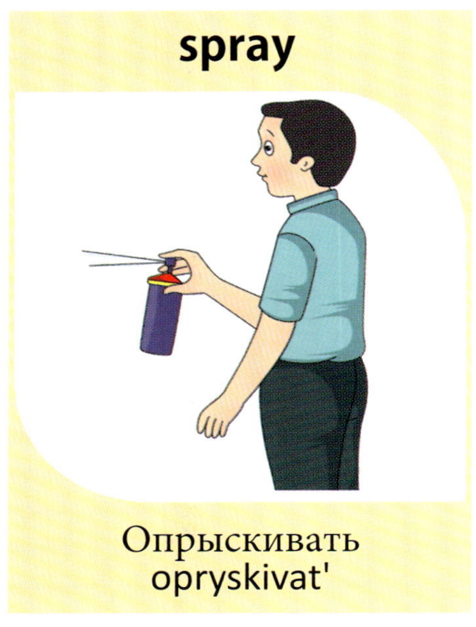

Опрыскивать
opryskivat'

spread

Размазать
razmazyvat'

spring

Подпрыгивать
podprygivat'

sprinkle

Поливать
polivat'

spy

Шпионить
shpionit'

squash

Давить
davit'

squat

Присесть
prisest'

squeeze

Сжимать
szhimat'

stack

Складывать в стог
skladyvat' v stog

stamp

Ставить печать
stavit' pechat'

stand

Стоять
stoyat'

stand back

Отойти
otoyti

stand up

Встать
vstat'

stare

Глазеть
glazet'

start

Начинать
nachinat'

stay

Остаться
ostat'sya

stay away

Держаться подальше
derzhat'sya podal'she

steal

Воровать
vorovat'

steam

Варить
varit'

step

Наступать
nastupat'

stick

Клеить
kleit'

sting

Укусить
ukusit'

stink

Вонять
vonyat'

stir

Размешивать
razmeshivaat'

stitch

Вышивать
vyshivat'

stomp

Топать
topat'

stoop

Наклоняться
naklonyat'sya

stop

Останавливаться
ostanavlivat'sya

store

Хранить
khranit'

stretch

Растягивать
rastyagivat'

strike

Ударять
udaryat'

string

Нанизывать
nanizyvat'

stroke

Поглаживать
poglazhivat'

study

Исследовать
issledovat'

subtract

Вычесть
vychest'

support

Поддерживать
podderzhivat'

surf

Заниматься серфингом
znimat'sya serfingom

surprise

Удивлять
udivlyat'

swallow

Глотать
glotat'

sweat

Потеть
potet'

sweep

Подметать
podmetat'

swell

Опухать
opukhat'

swim

Плавать
plavat'

swing

Качаться
kachat'sya

swipe

Смахивать
smakhivat'

Tt

take

Брать
brat'

take off

Взлетать
vzletat'

talk

Говорить
govorit'

tame

Приручать
priruchit'

tap

Наступать
nastupat'

taste

Пробовать
probovat'

teach

Учить
uchit'

tear

Рвать
rvat'

tell

Рассказывать
rasskazyvat'

test

Тестировать
testirovat'

thank

Благодарить
blagodarit'

think

Думать
dumat'

thread

Продевать нитку
prodevat' nitku

throw

Бросать
brosat'

throw away

Выбрасывать
vybrasyvat'

tick

Отмечать
otmechat'

tickle

Щекотать
shchekotat'

tidy	**tie**	**tighten**
	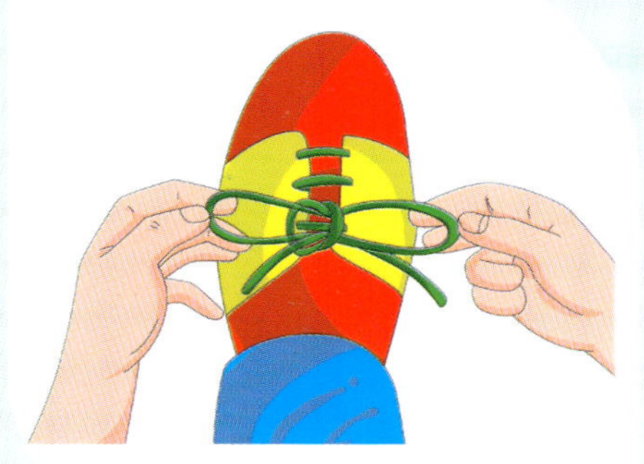	
Убирать ubirat'	Завязывать zavyazyvat'	Затягивать zatyagivat'
time	**tip**	**tiptoe**

Засекать zasekat'	Давать чаевые davat' chaevye	Красться krast'sya
toast	**toss**	**touch**

Поджаривать podzharivat'	Бросать brosat'	Трогать trogat'

touch down

Приземляться
prizemlyat'sya

tour

Гастролировать
gastrolirovat'

tow

Буксировать
buksirovat'

train

Тренироваться
trenirovat'sya

trap

Ловить
lovit'

travel

Путешествовать
puteshestvovat'

tremble

Дрожать
drozhat'

trick

Обманывать
obmanyvat'

trim

Подрезать
podrezat'

trot

Пускать рысью
puskat' rys'yu

try

Пытаться
pytat'sya

tug

Тянуть
tyanut'

turn

Поворачивать
povorachivat'

turn off

Выключать
vyklyuchat'

turn on

Включать
vklyuchat'

twinkle

Мерцать
mertsat'

twist

Скручивать
skuchivat'

type

Печатать
pechatat'

understand

Понимать
ponimat'

unload

Разгружать
razgruzhat'

unlock

Разблокировать
razblokirovat'

unpack

Распаковать
raspakovat'

untie

Развязать
razvyazat'

unwrap

Развернуть
razvernut'

upset

Расстраиваться
rasstraivat'sya

use

Использовать
ispol'zovat'

Vv

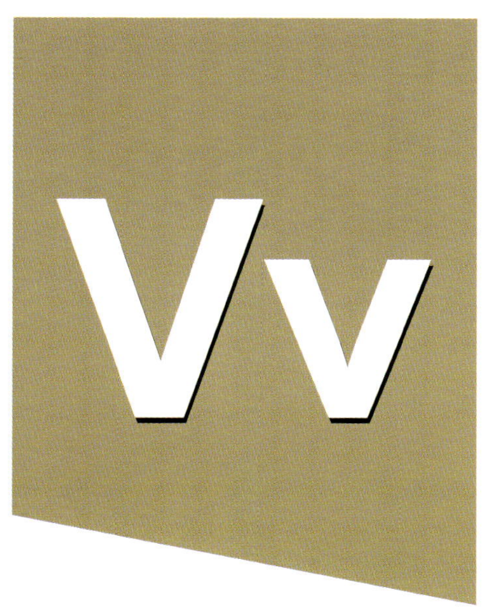

vacate

Освободить
osvobodit'

vacuum

Пылесосить
pylesosit'

value

Оценивать
otsenivat'

vanish

Исчезать
ischezat'

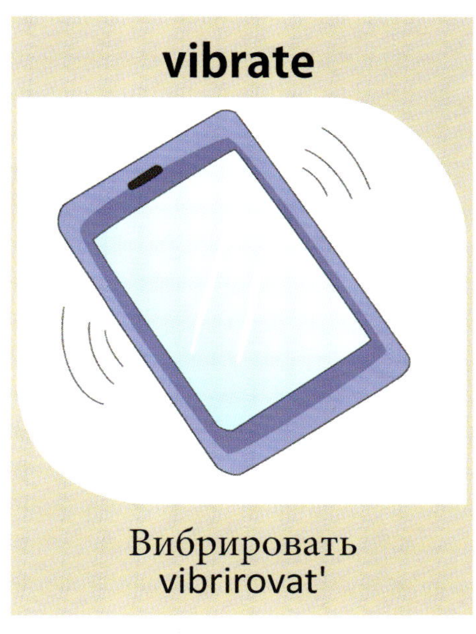

vibrate

Вибрировать
vibrirovat'

view

Смотреть
smotret'

visit

Посещать
poseshchat'

voice

Озвучить
ozvuchit'

volunteer

Вызываться добровольно
vyzyvat'sya dobrovol'no

vote

Голосовать
golosovat'

vow

Давать клятву
davat' klyatvu

Ww

waddle

Ходить вперевалку
khodit' vperevalku

wade

Переходить вброд
perekhodit' vbrod

wag

Вилять
vilyat'

wait

Ждать
zhdat'

wake

Просыпаться
prosypat'sya

wake up

Будить
budit'

walk

Ходить
hodit'

walk away

Уходить
uhodit'

wander

Бродить
brodit'

want

Хотеть
hotet'

warm

Согревать
sogrevat'

warn

Предупреждать
preduprezhdat'

wash

Стирать
stirat'

waste

Выбрасывать
vybrasyvat'

watch

Смотреть
smotret'

water

Поливать
polivat'

wave

Махать
mahat'

wear

Надеть
nadet'

wear out

Износить
iznosit'

weave

Ткать
tkat'

weed

Вырывать сорняки
vyryvat' sornyaki

weep

Плакать
plakat'

weigh

Взвешивать
vzveshivat'

welcome

Приветствовать
privetstvovat'

wet

Промокать
promokat'

wheel

Катать
katat'

whip

Взбивать
vzbivat'

whisper

Шептать
sheptat'

whistle

Свистеть
svistet'

win

Побеждать
pobezhdat'

wind

Заводить
zavodit'

wink

Подмигивать
podmigivat'

wipe

Вытирать
vytirat'

wish

Желать
zhelat'

wobble

Колебаться
kolebat'sya

wonder

Удивляться
udivljat'sya

work

Работать
rabotat'

work out

Упражняться
uprazhnjat'sya

worry

Волноваться
volnovat'sya

wrap

Сворачивать
svorachivat'

wrestle

Бороться
borot'sya

wriggle

Извиваться
izvivat'sja

wring

Отжать
otzhat'

write

Написать
napisat'

Xx

xerox

Делать копию
delat' kopiyu

x-ray

Делать рентген
delat' rentgen

Yy

yank

Дергать
dergat'

yap

Тявкать
tyavkat'

yawn

Зевать
zevat'

yearn

Жаждать
zhazhdat'

yell

Кричать
krichat'

yelp

Визжать
vizzhat'

yield

Приносить урожай
prinosit' urozhay

yodel

Петь йодлем
pet' yodlem

Zz

zigzag

Делать зигзаги
delat' zigzagi

zoom

Быстро ехать
bystro ehat'